"A wise person should have money in their head, but not in their heart."

- *Jonathan Swift*

"The more you chase money,
the harder it is to catch it."

- *Mike Tatum*

"A very rich person should leave his kids enough to do anything, but not enough to do nothing."

-*Warren Buffett*

"Don't tell me where your priorities are. Show me where you spend your money, and I'll tell you what they are."

- *James W. Frick*

"Investing should be more like watching paint dry or watching grass grow. If you want excitement, take $800 and go to Las Vegas."

- Paul Samuelson

"Wealth is the ability to fully
experience life."

- *Henry David Thoreau*

"The stock market is filled with individuals who know the price of everything, but the value of nothing."

- *Philip Fisher*

"The stock market is filled with opportunities for those who know how to wait."

- *Charlie Munger*

"The stock market is a device
for transferring money from
the impatient to the patient."

- *Warren Buffett*

"It's not how much money you make, but how much money you keep, how hard it works for you, and how many generations you keep it for."

- *Robert Kiyosaki*

"The true investor welcomes volatility."

- Benjamin Graham

"The best investment you can make is in yourself."

- *Warren Buffett*

"Wealth is not about having a
lot of money; it's about
having a lot of options."

- *Chris Rock*

"The rich invest in time, the poor invest in money."

- *Warren Buffett*

"Money, like emotions, is something you must control to keep your life on the right track."

- *Natasha Munson*

"Never spend your money
before you have earned it."

- Thomas Jefferson

"The greatest wealth is to live content with little."

– *Plato*

"You can't make a good deal
with a bad person."

-*Warren Buffett*

"Formal education will make you a living; self-education will make you a fortune."

- Jim Rohn

"It is not the man who has too little, but the man who craves more, that is poor."

— *Seneca*

"Money is usually attracted,
not pursued."

- *Jim Rohn*

"The goal isn't more money.
The goal is living life on your
terms."

- Chris Brogan

"The investor's chief problem, and even his worst enemy, is likely to be himself."

- *Benjamin Graham*

"Honesty is a very expensive gift. Don't expect it from cheap people."

-*Warren Buffett*

"The real measure of your wealth is how much you'd be worth if you lost all your money."

- *Bernard Meltzer*

"The only limit to our realization of tomorrow will be our doubts of today."

- Franklin D. Roosevelt

"Chains of habits are too light to be felt until they are too heavy to be broken."

-Warren Buffett

"The key to making money is to stay invested."

- *Suze Orman*

"It's not about how much
money you make, but how
much money you save."

- *Robert T. Kiyosaki*

"Every time you borrow
money, you're robbing your
future self."

- Nathan W. Morris

"Do not save what is left after spending, but spend what is left after saving."

-*Warren Buffett*

"Beware of little expenses. A small leak will sink a great ship."

- *Benjamin Franklin*

"Financial peace isn't the acquisition of stuff. It's learning to live on less than you make so you can give money back and have money to invest. You can't win until you do this."

- *Dave Ramsey*

"Wealth is not about having a lot of money; it's about having a lot of options."

- Chris Rock

"The more you learn, the
more you earn."

- *Warren Buffett*

"Don't tell me where your priorities are. Show me where you spend your money, and I'll tell you what they are."

- *James W. Frick*

"Investing should be more like watching paint dry or watching grass grow. If you want excitement, take $800 and go to Las Vegas."

- Paul Samuelson

"A person's main asset is themselves, so preserve and enhance yourself."

-*Warren Buffett*

"The stock market is filled with individuals who know the price of everything, but the value of nothing."

- Philip Fisher

"The stock market is filled with opportunities for those who know how to wait."

- Charlie Munger

"The stock market is a device
for transferring money from
the impatient to the patient."

- Warren Buffett

"It's not how much money you make, but how much money you keep, how hard it works for you, and how many generations you keep it for."

- *Robert Kiyosaki*

"The best investment you can make is in yourself."

- *Warren Buffett*

"Wealth is not about having a
lot of money; it's about
having a lot of options."

- *Chris Rock*

"The rich invest in time, the poor invest in money."

- *Warren Buffett*

"Money, like emotions, is something you must control to keep your life on the right track."

- *Natasha Munson*

"Never spend your money
before you have earned it."

- *Thomas Jefferson*

"The greatest wealth is to live content with little."

— *Plato*

"Formal education will make you a living; self-education will make you a fortune."

- Jim Rohn

"It is not the man who has
too little, but the man who
craves more, that is poor."

– *Seneca*

"Money is usually attracted,
not pursued."

- Jim Rohn

"The goal isn't more money. The goal is living life on your terms."

- *Chris Brogan*

"The real measure of your wealth is how much you'd be worth if you lost all your money."

- Bernard Meltzer

"The only limit to our
realization of tomorrow will
be our doubts of today."

- *Franklin D. Roosevelt*

"The key to making money is
to stay invested."

- *Suze Orman*

"It's not about how much money you make, but how much money you save."

- *Robert T. Kiyosaki*

"Every time you borrow money, you're robbing your future self."

- Nathan W. Morris

"Beware of little expenses. A small leak will sink a great ship."

- Benjamin Franklin

"The stock market is filled with individuals who know the price of everything, but the value of nothing."

- Benjamin Graham

"The intelligent investor is a realist who sells to optimists and buys from pessimists."

- Benjamin Graham

"Your true inner happiness does not come from the material things of this world."

- Steve jobs

"The investor's chief problem,
and even his worst enemy, is
likely to be himself."

- *Benjamin Graham*

"In the short run, the market is a voting machine, but in the long run, it is a weighing machine."

- *Benjamin Graham*

"An investment in knowledge pays the best interest."

- *Benjamin Graham*

"If a rich man is proud of his
wealth, he should not be
praised until it is known how
he employs it."

- Socrates